THE OXPECKER AND THE GIRAFFE

I NEED YOU AND YOU NEED ME

Written by
Patrick Fitzpatrick

Illustrated by
Tim Newcombe

Published and distributed by

CREATION
BOOK PUBLISHERS

www.creationbookpublishers.com

Dedicated to my wife and five children, because
I need you and you need me.—P.F.

For my parents and sister, for always being there.—T.N.

About the Author

Patrick Fitzpatrick earned a BS in biology from Wheaton College and an MS in biology from Georgia State University. He has been a biology teacher and high school administrator since 1987, inspiring thousands of kids to marvel at God's creative genius.

About the Illustrator

Tim Newcombe holds a Bachelor of Communication Design specializing in Graphic Design. Presently he is a full-time Graphic Designer for *Creation Ministries International*.

ISBN: 978-1-921-64308-8

Third printing

Book design by Tim Newcombe. Printed by Tien Wah Press.

For information on creation/evolution issues and materials for all ages, visit:

CREATION.com

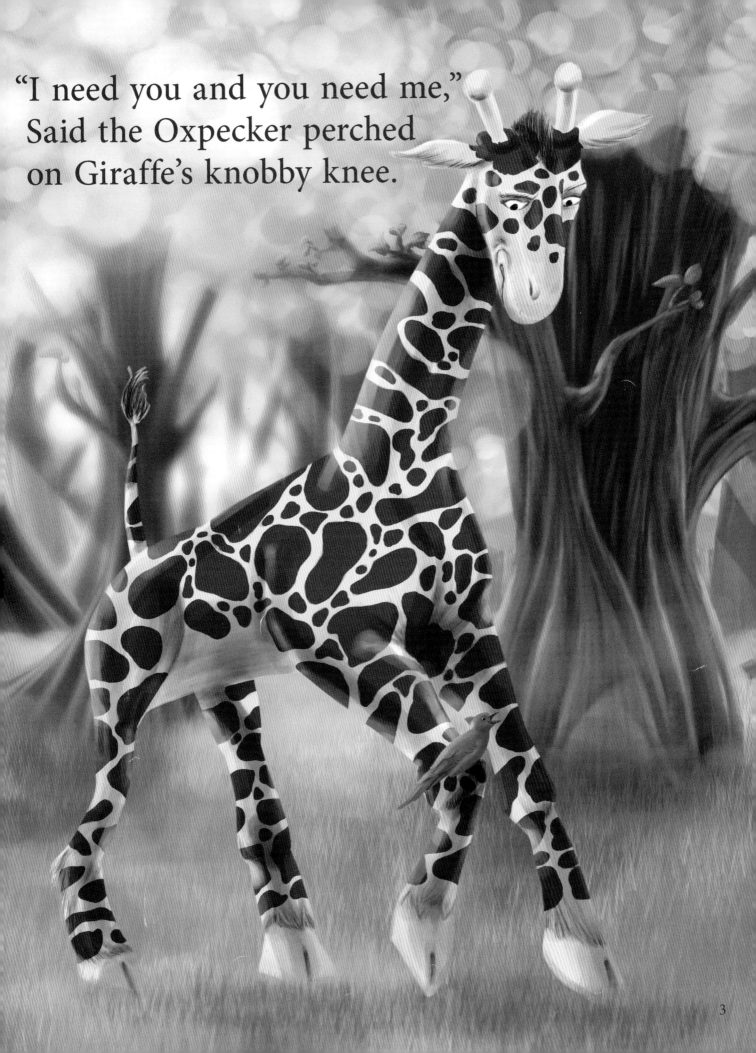

"I need you and you need me,"
Said the Oxpecker perched
on Giraffe's knobby knee.

3

Glaring at him, Giraffe frowned,
"I do not need you. Please get down."

4

"You're always climbing on my skin.
Your company is wearing thin.
You are nothing but a pest.
Fly away and let me rest."

"But I need you and you need me.
Let me speak and you will see.
I hang around all day and night,
Picking every thing in sight.
I pick, pick, pick, pick, pick, pick, pick –
I'm always looking for a tick.
I eat the bugs that drink you dry,
On your neck, your back, your thigh."

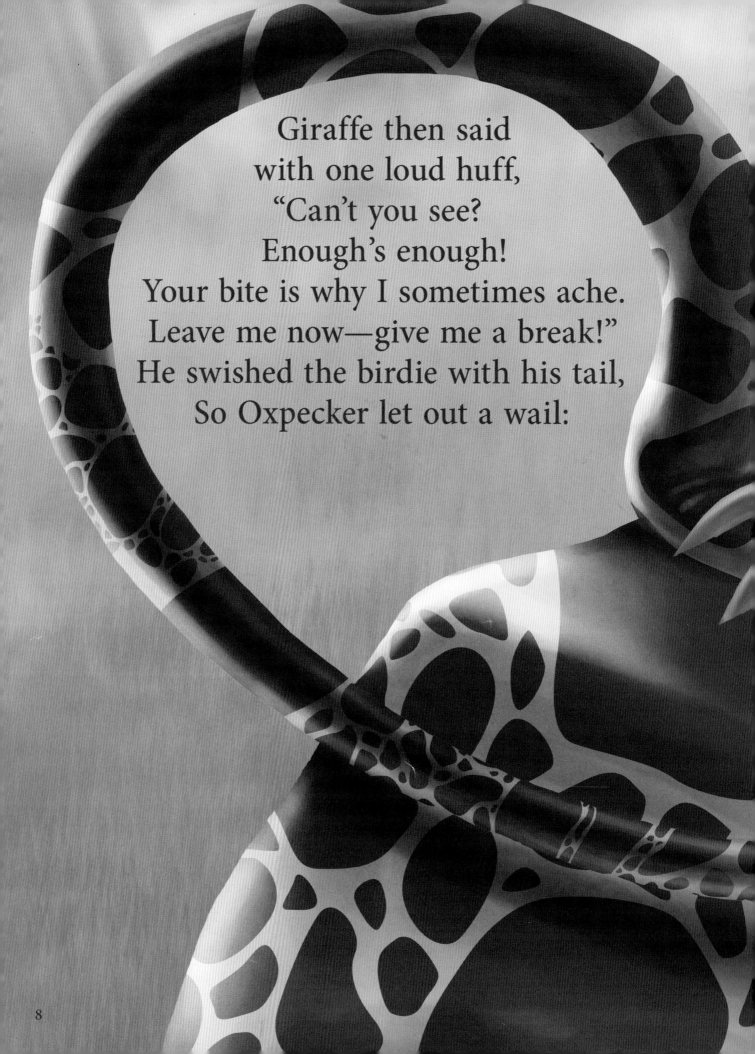

Giraffe then said
with one loud huff,
"Can't you see?
Enough's enough!
Your bite is why I sometimes ache.
Leave me now—give me a break!"
He swished the birdie with his tail,
So Oxpecker let out a wail:

"Easy does it, dear old friend;
Listen well and comprehend.
It's true that sometimes I may bite,
When I am hunting for a mite.
So if my beak hurts you a tad,
Please know the good outweighs the bad."

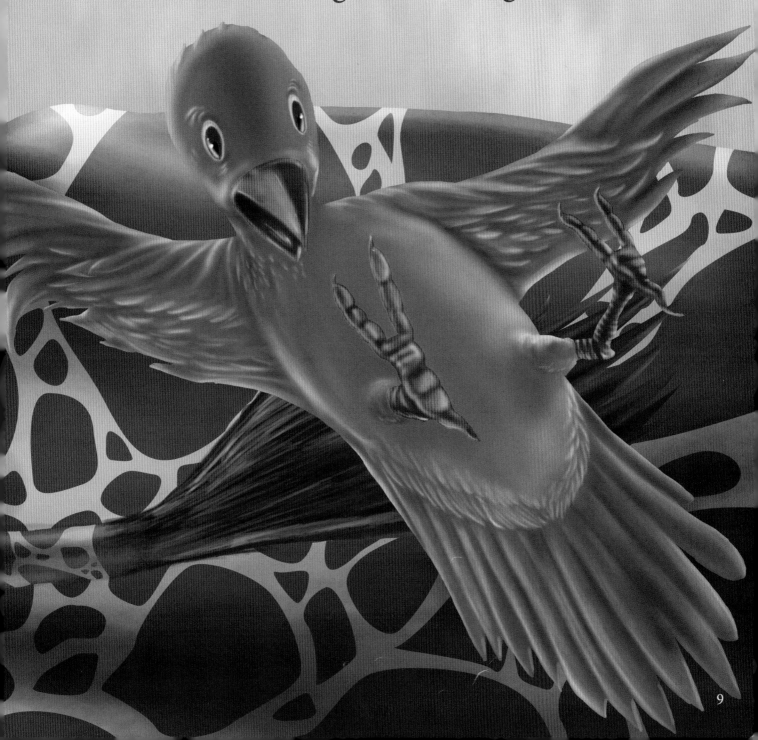

"I *don't* need you…that makes me laugh!
Remember, I'm a big giraffe.
No other beast on earth's as tall.
I am taller than them all."

"Look at me. Look at my size.
No other beast has stronger thighs.
My kick is swift and packed with power.
From it even lions cower."
Giraffe continued in his pride,
"I'm also great on the inside.
Listen to my large chest pound;
I have the biggest heart around."

Oxpecker peered into his eyes,
And said, "It's true, you win the prize.
You are the tallest on the plain,
And next to me, a great big brain.
But there is still one thing that's true,
You need me and I need you."

"Let me tell you," chirped the bird.
"Listen to my every word.
Every day the bugs return,
And that should give you some concern.
I conduct a daily hunt,
Perching on your back or front.
I even crawl inside your ears.
You really don't have any fears,
Of getting sick from parasites,
like fleas and ticks and even mites."

"When I'm busy with young hatching,
You spend much more time a-scratching."

"Your tail goes swish, your shoulder shrugs,
Your body shakes from all the bugs."

"But when I'm busy at my work,
you no longer go berserk.
You relax within my care,
When I'm hunting in your hair,
For all the tiny bugs, like fleas,
That can carry bad disease."

Giraffe then said, "I do not know.
I need to ask my friend Rhino."

He walked across the grassy plain.
The wind was blowing through his mane.
Hyenas, laughing, stepped aside,
From his long and graceful stride.

Giraffe then climbed upon a knoll;
From there he spied a waterhole.
Flamingos fed and elephants played,
Gazelles were grazing in the shade.

Soon he saw his friend Rhino,
Feeding near Cape Buffalo.
Giraffe saw birds on both their backs,
So he said, "I want the facts.
Should I let this bird hang out?
Please erase my every doubt."

"Do I really need this bird?"

Rhino answered, "Rest assured.
We need them and they need us.
Why the worry? Why the fuss?
God has made us by design,
So our lives must intertwine."

Cape Buffalo chewed on his cud,
And stomped his split hooves in the mud.
Then he spoke in his low voice,
"Frankly we don't have a choice.
Don't you see, my friend Giraffe?
You and the bird are only half,
Of one big whole that God has made,
You should be glad the bird has stayed."

Giraffe smiled and faced the bird,
And then he said a single word.
"Thanks." That's all—that's all he said,
As Oxpecker crawled upon his head.
He smiled again. He understood.
Giraffe could see that it was good.
"You feed on all the things you pick.
Your work keeps me from getting sick.
There is a reason. I can see,
I need you and you need me."

Giraffe continued with his lunch,
Eating green leaves by the bunch.
He thanked God, as he ate a limb,
For the bird that feeds on him.